Perfecting The Hunt: Discovering More Real Estate Leads

Stephen Zochowski

Published by:

SGZ Properties, LLC

37539 Landis Ave, Zephyrhills, FL

33541

First SGZ Properties, LLC paperback edition August 2023

SGZ Properties, LLC

Perfecting The Hunt: Discovering More Real Estate Leads

Dedication

I dedicate this book to God. My prayer is that His Holy Spirit will draw all who read it to a clear understanding of the good news described herein.

Acknowledgment

God for His Word and wonderful care for His children.
My wife of 30 years, for every year of marriage and how
she loved me and supported my many endeavors. You are
my anchor and the first reason for living by faith.
Paul and Linda for pointing out my need for a relationship
with Jesus and their lifelong commitment to teaching the
firm foundation of Biblical faith in God. May God keep
you healthy in mind, body and spirit.
Dr. Randolph and all my brothers and sisters at Fellowship
Church. Their care for each other and their love for God
inspired me to study diligently in writing this book.
My siblings, nephews and nieces, their spouses and their
children, for the examples they all are to me as their
brother, uncle and great uncle to live life with integrity,
love and joy. I appreciate each one of you and your
involvement in each other's lives.
Jim and Amanda for hiring me to work for them and having
faith in my ability to do a good job for them. My position
has been a Godsend to me; I am very grateful to you both.
My friends in real estate and the automotive industries. You
have all openly shown your integrity in business practices
and helped me to shoot for a higher standard in life.
All the folks at Real America's Voice for the inspiration I
received and the truth they broadcast to and of all patriots
around the globe. Our world needs to hear the truth shouted
from the highest mountain!

CONTENTS

About the Author

Stephen Zochowski is a patriot of the state of the United States of America. He married in the state of Indiana, USA and is currently a resident of the state of Florida, USA.

The author is available to deliver keynote presentations to appropriate audiences. For rates and availability, don't hesitate to get in touch with the author directly at:

To order more books, please visit:

www.amazon.com

Finally, if you have found Wisdom through this book, the best thing you could ever do is pass that knowledge on and be a witness to others.

Page Blank Intentionally

Foreword

In the world of real estate, where dreams find homes and futures are shaped, Stephen Zochowski's "Perfecting The Hunt: Discovering More Real Estate Leads" emerges as a beacon of guidance and purpose. As a devout Christian and devoted husband, Stephen infuses this book with a profound intention—to not only share strategies for lead generation but to glorify God through its impact.

Within these pages, Stephen's expertise intertwines seamlessly with his faith-driven mission. With each chapter meticulously outlined, readers are invited on a journey that transcends business acumen. The intricacies of lead generation are expertly dissected. Still, at the heart of it all lies a deeper purpose – a purpose rooted in Stephen's belief that success is a partnership between human diligence and divine grace.

Stephen's Christian values are woven into the fabric of this book, reminding us that our professional endeavors can be vessels for spiritual alignment. In a concise yet impactful manner, each chapter unravels techniques, strategies, and insights while simultaneously illuminating the author's unwavering commitment to a higher calling.

As you engage with the outlined chapters, remember that you're not just absorbing knowledge; you're embracing a philosophy that aims to elevate your business acumen and your spirit. Through Stephen's words, God's presence is invoked, reminding us that our actions—no matter how practical or professional—can be conduits for the divine.

Stephen Zochowski's journey unfolds within these pages, a journey that seeks to magnify God's glory through every real estate transaction, every connection made, and every lead generated. This foreword stands as a tribute to Stephen's intention—a reminder that through faith, knowledge, and purposeful action, we can craft success that echoes in eternity.

All scripture references are from the King James Bible.

With faith as our guide,

Chapter 1 –

Introduction: Understanding Real Estate Leads

In this chapter, we will explore the concept of real estate leads and understand why focusing on leads is crucial in the real estate industry. Let's get started!

Definition of Real Estate Leads

Real estate leads refer to individuals or organizations that express interest or show potential in buying, selling, renting, or investing in real estate properties. These leads typically provide contact information, such as names, phone numbers, and email addresses, allowing real estate professionals to follow up and engage with them.

Leads can come from various sources, including websites, social media platforms, referrals, open houses, and marketing campaigns. They can be categorized into two types:

1. Buyer Leads Individuals or organizations looking to purchase real estate properties for personal use or investment purposes.

2. Seller Leads Individuals or organizations looking to sell their real estate properties.

Why Focusing on Leads is Crucial in Real Estate

Focusing on leads is essential for several reasons in the real estate industry:

1. Business Growth: Generating a consistent flow of leads is vital for real estate professionals to grow their businesses. Quality leads can turn into clients, leading to successful transactions and increased revenue.

2. Conversion Opportunities: Leads provide conversion opportunities, allowing real estate professionals to nurture these prospects and convert them into clients. By dedicating time and resources to lead generation, real estate professionals can increase their chances of closing deals.

3. Competitive Advantage: In a competitive real estate market, having a robust lead generation strategy gives professionals a competitive edge. By proactively reaching out to potential clients, real estate professionals can establish relationships and position themselves ahead of their competition.

4. Targeted Marketing Efforts: Effective lead generation allows real estate professionals to focus their marketing efforts on a specific target audience. By understanding the preferences and needs of their leads, professionals can tailor their marketing messages and strategies to attract the right clients.

5. Increasing Network and Referrals: Leads can also contribute to expanding a real estate professional's network. By establishing meaningful connections with leads, professionals can tap into their networks and gain referrals, leading to a steady stream of new leads.

In summary, real estate leads are individuals or organizations interested in buying, selling, renting, or investing in real estate properties. Focusing on leads is crucial in the real estate industry as it leads to business growth, conversion opportunities, a competitive advantage, targeted marketing efforts, and increased networking possibilities.

The driving force of your real estate business needs to have a solid foundation. Hunting, in ancient days, was the only way a man could eat. God placed a significant importance on his provision to man by providing animals for our use. Historically, men (and women) have been hunters/gatherers. The first animal was sacrificed by God to give us an example of the proper use of the 'Hunt' and for atonement. More on this subject later.

In the next chapter, we will delve deeper into various lead-generation strategies and explore effective techniques for generating real estate leads.

Chapter 2 –

The Foundation - Building a Solid Network

In this chapter, we will explore the significance of networking in the real estate industry. We will discuss techniques for effective networking and how to utilize connections to generate leads. Let's dive in!

The Importance of Networking

Networking plays a critical role in the real estate industry for several reasons:

1. Building Relationships: Networking is basically about building relationships with other professionals, potential clients, and industry influencers. These relationships often result in referrals, partnerships, and valuable connections that can contribute to generating leads. The first and most important relationship you need to establish is with God. Do you know Him? Have you accepted his free gift of salvation through Jesus Christ, His son?

2. Trust and Credibility: Through networking, real estate professionals can establish trust and credibility within their industry. When people know and trust you, they are more likely to recommend your services, increasing your chances of acquiring quality leads. People trust you if you are trustworthy. God can be trusted. In the King James Bible, trust is mentioned 134 times. In 2 Samuel 22:3, David wrote, "The God of my rock; in him will I trust: *he is* my shield, and the horn of my salvation, my high tower, and my refuge, my savior; thou savest me from violence." Later in the same chapter, David wrote in verse 31, "*As for* God, his way *is* perfect; the word of the LORD *is* tried: he *is* a buckler to all them that trust in him." Whom do you trust, dear reader?

The apostle Paul wrote in his first letter to Timothy 4:10, "For therefore we both labour and suffer reproach, because we trust in the living God, who is the Saviour of all men, especially of those that believe."

A relationship with God can enhance your ability to have credibility for your clients and potential clients.

3. Knowledge Exchange: Networking provides an opportunity to exchange knowledge and expertise among industry professionals. By participating in events, conferences, or online communities, you can learn from others and stay updated with the latest trends and best practices.

The ultimate knowledge we can gain is found through God's word, the Bible. A head knowledge can only get you so far in the business world. First, you must have a heart knowledge of Jesus. This is found woven throughout the biblical text. Specifically found in the book of Proverbs in the Old Testament and John in the New Testament. One hundred seventy-two times in the King James Bible, knowledge is taught.

Proverbs 9:10: "The fear of the LORD *is* the beginning of wisdom: and the knowledge of the holy *is* understanding."

Romans 11:33: "O the depth of the riches both of the wisdom and knowledge of God! How unsearchable *are* his judgments, and his ways past finding out!"

God has knowledge for you. Through the Apostle Peter's second letter, he tells us seven times about this knowledge. The knowledge of God and His son, our Lord Jesus Christ. 2 Peter 1:2-3, 5-6, 8; 2:20 and 3:18.

"Grace and peace be multiplied unto you through the knowledge of God, and of Jesus our Lord,

According as his divine power hath given unto us all things that *pertain* unto life and godliness, through the knowledge of him that hath called us to glory and virtue:

And beside this, giving all diligence, add to your faith virtue; and to virtue knowledge;

And to knowledge temperance; and to temperance patience; and to patience godliness;

For if these things be in you, and abound, they make *you that ye shall* neither *be* barren nor unfruitful in the knowledge of our Lord Jesus Christ.

For if after they have escaped the pollutions of the world through the knowledge of the Lord and Saviour Jesus Christ, they are again entangled therein and overcome, the latter end is worse with them than the beginning.

But grow in grace and *in* the knowledge of our Lord and Saviour Jesus Christ. To him *be* glory both now and forever. Amen."

4. Access to New Opportunities: Effective networking opens doors to opportunities that might otherwise remain undiscovered. These opportunities can include joint ventures, partnerships, or collaborations that can lead to a wider reach and increased lead generation.

Techniques for Effective Networking

To make the most of networking opportunities, consider the following techniques:

1. Attending Industry Events: Attend local real estate conferences, seminars, and networking events to meet other professionals and potential clients. Be prepared with business cards and engage in meaningful conversations to build connections.

2. Joining Professional Organizations: Join real estate associations or professional organizations that align with your niche or target market. These organizations offer networking opportunities and resources to enhance your industry presence.

3. Utilizing Social Media: Leverage social media platforms, such as LinkedIn, Facebook groups, or real estate forums, to connect with other professionals and engage in industry-related discussions. Share valuable content and actively participate in relevant conversations to establish yourself as an authority figure.

4. Hosting Events or Workshops: Organize your own networking events, workshops, or webinars to gather professionals and potential clients in a single location. These workshops and events allow you to showcase your expertise and build relationships in a more controlled environment.

Chapter 3 – Exploring Digital Marketing

In this chapter, we will delve into various digital marketing strategies that can be effective in generating real estate leads. We will explore techniques such as website optimization, social media marketing, email marketing, online advertising, and utilizing lead generation platforms and real estate portals. Let's get started!

Website and Search Engine Optimization (SEO)

A well-designed and optimized website is crucial for generating real estate leads. Consider the following strategies:

1. Mobile-Friendly Design: Ensure your website is mobile-friendly to cater to the growing number of users accessing the internet through mobile devices.

2. User-Friendly Experience: Provide an intuitive and easy-to-navigate user experience on your website. Optimize page loading speed and ensure the information is easily accessible.

3. High-Quality Content: Produce high-quality and informative content on your website, such as property listings, market reports, neighborhood guides, and blog articles. Quality content can improve your website's visibility in online search results.

4. Search Engine Optimization (SEO): Implement SEO techniques to improve your website's visibility in search engine results by optimizing page titles, Meta descriptions, and headers and using relevant keywords throughout your content.

Social Media Marketing

Social media platforms provide an excellent opportunity to reach a wider audience and engage with potential leads. Consider the following strategies for social media marketing:

1. Establish a Presence: Create professional profiles on popular social media platforms such as Facebook, Instagram, Twitter, and LinkedIn. Ensure your profiles are complete, showcase your services, and provide contact information.

2. Content Strategy: Develop a content strategy to share relevant and engaging content on social media, like property listings, market updates, home buying tips, neighborhood highlights, and success stories.

3. Engage with Your Audience: Actively engage with your audience by responding to comments, messages, and inquiries promptly. Encourage conversation, answer questions, and leverage social media features like polls, quizzes, and live videos.

Email Marketing and Newsletters

Utilize email marketing to nurture leads and stay in touch with potential clients. Consider the following email marketing strategies:

1. Lead Capture: Place lead capture forms on your website, allowing visitors to subscribe to your newsletter or receive updates about new listings and market trends.

2. Personalized Communication: Segment your email list based on interests, preferences, and stage in the buying or selling process in order to personalize your emails and provide relevant information.

3. Valuable Content: Provide valuable content in your emails, such as property spotlights, market reports, tips for buyers and sellers, and upcoming events or webinars to establish credibility and keep your audience engaged.

Online Ads and Pay-Per-Click (PPC) Campaigns

Online advertising and PPC campaigns can be effective in reaching a targeted audience. Consider the following strategies:

1. Google Ads: Utilize Google Ads to display ads when users search for relevant keywords related to real estate in your target market. Optimize your ads to appear at the top of search engine results.

2. Social Media Ads: Leverage platforms like Facebook and Instagram to create targeted ad campaigns. Utilize demographic and interest targeting to reach potential leads.

Using Lead Generation Platforms and Real Estate Portals

Utilize lead generation platforms and real estate portals to access a large pool of potential leads. Consider the following strategies:

1. Zillow, Realtor.com, and Other Portals: List your properties on popular real estate portals to increase visibility and reach a wider audience. Be sure to optimize your listings with high-quality photos, detailed descriptions, and accurate information.

2. Lead Generation Platforms: Consider using lead generation platforms like Zoho, HubSpot, or Bold Leads to access pre-qualified leads and automate lead nurturing processes.

In conclusion, digital marketing can play a vital role in generating real estate leads. By optimizing your website, utilizing social media marketing, implementing email marketing strategies, running online ads, and utilizing lead generation platforms, you can attract and engage with potential clients effectively.

All of these techniques are feasible for realtors today and far into the future. Keep in mind that the ultimate provider is God for the believer. Have you decided to follow Jesus? Do you know how to believe? Romans 10:9-10 tells you how "That if thou shalt confess with thy mouth the Lord Jesus, and shalt believe in thine heart that God hath raised him from the dead, thou shalt be saved. For with the heart man believeth unto righteousness; and with the mouth confession is made unto salvation."

In the next chapter, we will explore the importance of providing exceptional customer service and the impact it can have on generating real estate leads and securing referrals.

Chapter 4 –

Traditional Marketing Methods

In this chapter, we will explore traditional marketing methods that can still be effective in generating real estate leads. We will discuss techniques such as direct mail, outdoor advertising, newspaper and magazine ads, and radio and TV commercials. Let's dive in!

Direct Mail

Direct mail involves sending physical promotional materials, such as postcards, brochures, or letters, to a targeted audience. Consider the following strategies for effective direct mail campaigns:

1. Targeted Mailing Lists: Use targeted mailing lists to reach individuals who are more likely to be interested in real estate. Homeowners, renters, or specific demographics based on location, income, or other relevant factors are all included in it. Targets are needed for practice in hunting. To Perfect your Hunt for leads, this type of campaigning will sharpen your skills.

2. Compelling Design and Messaging: Create eye-catching designs and compelling messages that highlight your unique selling propositions and benefits to the recipient. Include a call-to-action that prompts them to take the next step, such as visiting your website or calling your office. God uses messengers to further His word. Will you be His messenger?

3. Personalization: Personalize your direct mail pieces whenever possible. Address recipients by their names and consider tailoring the messaging based on their specific needs or interests.

Outdoor Advertising

Outdoor advertising refers to promotional messages displayed in public places, such as billboards, bus shelters, or digital signage. Consider the following strategies for effective outdoor advertising:

1. Strategic Placement: Choose high-traffic areas or key locations in your target market to place your outdoor advertisements. Busy intersections, commuter routes, or arcas near popular shopping centers are the best choices in this regard.

2. Eye-Catching Design: Ensure your outdoor advertisements have a clear and attention-grabbing design. Use bold colors, concise messaging, and high-quality images that resonate with your target audience.

3. Clear Contact Information: Include your contact information, such as phone number, website, or social media handles, on the outdoor advertisements. Make it easy for potential leads to get in touch with you.

Newspaper and Magazine Ads

Newspaper and magazine ads provide an opportunity to reach a local audience and generate real estate leads. Consider the following strategies for effective print advertising:

1. Targeted Publications: Advertise in newspapers or magazines that cater to your target market. Consider local publications or those with a specific focus, such as real estate or lifestyle magazines.

2. Compelling Headlines and Captivating Content: Craft attention-grabbing headlines that pique the interest of potential leads. Include captivating content that highlights your unique offerings and compels readers to act.

3. Calls-to-Action: Include a strong call-to-action in your ads, such as visiting your website, calling for a free consultation, or attending an open house event. Make it clear what steps readers should take to engage with you.

Radio and TV Commercials

Radio and TV commercials can effectively reach a wider audience and create brand awareness. Consider the following strategies for effective audio and video advertising:

1. Clear and Memorable Messages: Craft clear and memorable messages that convey your unique selling propositions and benefits. Use storytelling techniques to engage and connect with the audience.

2. Consistent Branding: Ensure your commercials have consistent branding elements, such as your logo, colors, and tagline. Well focused branding helps in building brand recognition and association.

3. Time of Day and Programming Selection: Consider the time of day and programming selection when airing your commercials. Target specific time slots or programs that attract your desired audience, such as morning drive-time radio shows or popular TV shows.

In conclusion, traditional marketing methods can still be effective in generating real estate leads. By utilizing direct mail campaigns, outdoor advertising, newspaper and magazine ads, and radio and TV commercials strategically, you can reach a wider audience and attract potential clients.

In the next chapter, we will explore the importance of exceptional customer service and the impact it can have on generating real estate leads and securing referrals.

Chapter 5 –

Event Hosting and Participation

In this chapter, we will explore the importance of hosting and participating in events as a strategy for generating real estate leads. We will discuss techniques such as hosting open houses, participating in property fairs and community events, and networking at industry conferences and seminars. Let's dive in!

Hosting Open Houses

Open houses are an effective way to showcase properties and engage with potential buyers. Consider the following strategies for hosting successful open houses:

1. Preparation: Prepare the property to create an inviting and welcoming atmosphere. Clean and declutter the space, stage it appropriately, and ensure everything is in good condition.

2. Marketing and Promotion: Advertise the open house through various channels, such as your website, social media platforms, online listings, and local publications. Use captivating descriptions and high-quality photos to attract potential buyers.

3. In-Person Engagement: Interact with visitors during the open house to understand their needs, answer questions, and provide additional information about the property. Offer refreshments and create a positive and memorable experience.

Participating in Property Fairs and Community Events

Participating in property fairs and community events allows you to connect with potential buyers and sellers. Consider the following strategies for effective participation:

1. Research and Planning: Identify relevant property fairs and community events in your target market. Research the demographics of attendees and align your participation accordingly.

2. Booth or Table Setup: Create an attractive and informative booth or table set up at the event. Display your branding materials, property listings, and promotional materials, and engage with visitors to generate leads.

3. Active Engagement: Actively engage with event attendees by striking up conversations, answering questions, and collecting contact information. Follow up with leads after the event to nurture the relationship.

Networking at Industry Conferences and Seminars

Attending industry conferences and seminars provides valuable networking opportunities with other professionals and potential clients. Consider the following strategies for effective networking:

1. Research and Selectivity: Choose conferences and seminars that align with your interests, expertise, or target market. Research the speakers, attendees, and topics to ensure they will be beneficial for your networking goals.

2. Active Participation: Actively participate in sessions, workshops, and networking events during conferences or seminars. Ask questions, share your knowledge, and engage in meaningful conversations with fellow attendees.

3. Follow-Up and Relationship Building: After the event, follow up with your new contacts to further build the relationship. Send personalized emails, connect on social media, or even schedule one-on-one meetings to discuss potential collaboration or business opportunities.

In conclusion, hosting open houses, participating in property fairs and community events, and networking at industry conferences and seminars are effective strategies for generating real estate leads. By showcasing properties, engaging with potential buyers and sellers, and connecting with other professionals, you can expand your network and attract potential clients.

In the next chapter, we will explore the role of exceptional customer service in generating leads and securing referrals in the real estate industry.

Chapter 6 –
Cultivating Referral Systems

In this chapter, we will explore the importance of cultivating referral systems to generate real estate leads. We will discuss strategies such as creating beneficial relationships with past clients, working with estate attorneys/ divorce attorneys, and building relationships with financial institutions. Let's begin!

Creating Beneficial Relationships with Past Clients

Past clients can be a valuable source of referral leads. By maintaining strong relationships with them, you can encourage them to refer their friends, family, and colleagues to your real estate services. Consider the following strategies:

1. Stay in Touch: Regularly stay in touch with your past clients through email newsletters, personalized messages, or social media interactions. Keep them informed about market updates, relevant news, and any special events or promotions you may have.

2. Provide Exceptional Service: Ensure that your past clients had a positive experience when working with you. Going above and beyond their expectations will make them more likely to refer you to others.

3. Request Referrals: Don't hesitate to ask your past clients for referrals. Let them know that you are actively seeking new clients and would appreciate their recommendations. Offering incentives, such as discounts or gift cards, can also motivate them to refer you to their connections.

Working with Estate Attorneys, Divorce Attorneys, etc.

Establishing relationships with professionals in related industries can lead to a steady stream of referral leads. Professionals like estate attorneys or divorce attorneys often come across clients who have real estate needs. Consider the following strategies:

1. Connect and Collaborate: Reach out to estate attorneys, divorce attorneys, and other professionals who may come into contact with clients needing real estate assistance. Offer to provide educational resources or be available for consultations to understand their client's needs better.

Chapter 7 –

Cold Calling and Door-Knocking

In this chapter, we will explore the art of cold calling and door-knocking as strategies for generating real estate leads. We will discuss effective techniques for both, as well as ways to overcome fear and handle rejections. Let's get started!

The Art of Cold Calling

Cold calling involves reaching out to potential leads or prospects over the phone with whom you have had no prior connection. Although it can be intimidating, it can be a powerful tool for generating real estate leads. Consider the following strategies:

1. Preparation is Key: Before making any cold calls, research your leads and gather information about their needs, preferences, and current real estate situation. It will help you tailor your conversation and offers to their specific circumstances.

2. Refine Your Pitch: Develop a concise and compelling script that highlights the value you can provide. Focus on how you can solve their problems or meet their needs. Also, be prepared with answers to common objections or questions.

3. Personalize When Possible: Whenever possible, personalize your cold calls by mentioning any common connections, shared interests, or recent market trends that may be relevant to the prospect. It shows that you've done your homework and are genuinely interested in their situation.

4. Follow-Up: If a prospect expresses interest or requests more information, make sure to follow up with the requested details promptly. Being responsive and proactive can build trust and increase the chances of converting a lead into a client.

Effective Strategies for Door-Knocking

Door-knocking involves physically visiting potential leads or neighborhoods in person to engage with homeowners and generate real estate leads. Consider the following strategies for effective door-knocking:

1. Be Prepared: Before heading out for door-knocking, research the neighborhood and gather market information that may be valuable to homeowners. Prepare marketing materials such as brochures, business cards, or flyers to leave with interested individuals.

2. Use a Friendly and Approachable Approach: Approach each door with a friendly and professional demeanor. Introduce yourself, explain your purpose, and offer assistance or information about the local real estate market. Engage in a conversation and listen to the homeowner's needs and concerns.

3. Provide Value: Offer something of value to homeowners, such as a neighborhood market report, home valuation, or tips on increasing property value. Providing useful information can help build trust and establish yourself as a knowledgeable resource.

Chapter 8 –

Farming a Niche Audience

In this chapter, we will explore the concept of farming a niche audience as a strategy for generating real estate leads. We will discuss techniques such as identifying niche markets, implementing targeting strategies, and building a strong presence and reputation within the niche. Let's begin!

Identifying Niche Markets

Niche markets are specific segments within the real estate industry that have unique needs, preferences, or characteristics. By focusing your efforts on a niche audience, you can better tailor your marketing strategies and attract highly targeted leads. Consider the following strategies for identifying niche markets:

1. Research Local Trends: Conduct research to identify any emerging or underserved market segments in your area. Look for factors such as demographics, lifestyle preferences, or specific needs that may present opportunities for niche marketing.

2. Assess Your Expertise: Evaluate your skills, knowledge, and interests to identify areas where you can specialize. Consider your personal experiences, certifications, or unique selling propositions that can help you stand out within a particular niche.

3. Analyze Market Data: Analyze market data, such as sales trends, inventory levels, or price fluctuations, to identify potential niche markets. Look for segments that may have different buying patterns, interests, or demands compared to the broader market.

Implementing Targeting Strategies

Once you've identified your niche audience, it's important to implement targeted marketing strategies to reach and engage with them effectively. Consider the following strategies:

1. Create Relevant Content: Develop content that speaks directly to the interests and needs of your niche audience, which can include blog articles, social media posts, videos, or downloadable resources that address specific topics or challenges related to the niche.

2. Utilize Online Targeting: Leverage online advertising platforms, such as Facebook Ads or Google Ads, to target your niche audience based on their demographics, interests, or online behavior. It allows you to reach a highly specific audience with your marketing messages.

3. Form Strategic Partnerships: Identify other professionals or businesses that cater to the same niche audience and form strategic partnerships. It can involve referring clients to each other, co-hosting events or webinars, or collaborating on marketing initiatives that benefit both parties.

Building a Strong Presence and Reputation within the Niche

To effectively farm a niche audience, it's essential to establish a strong presence and reputation within that specific market segment. Consider the following strategies:

1. Consistency and Expertise: Consistently demonstrate your expertise and knowledge within the niche through your marketing materials, online content, and interactions with clients. It builds trust and positions you as a credible resource.

2. Engage in Community Involvement: Get involved in local community activities, organizations, or events that are relevant to your niche market. It helps you build connections, expand your network, and increase your visibility within the community.

3. Seek Client Testimonials: Encourage satisfied clients within your niche market to provide testimonials or reviews that highlight their positive experiences working with you. This social proof can significantly impact your reputation and attract new leads.

In conclusion, farming a niche audience involves identifying specific market segments, implementing targeted marketing strategies, and building a strong presence and reputation. By focusing your efforts on a niche, you can better cater to the unique needs and preferences of your audience, positioning yourself as an expert within that niche and attracting highly targeted leads.

In the next chapter, we will explore the importance of leveraging online reviews.

Chapter 9 –

Utilizing Technology

In this chapter, we will explore the importance of utilizing technology in the real estate industry. We will discuss the benefits of customer relationship management (CRM) systems, automation tools for lead generation and nurturing, and real estate investment software. Let's dive in!

Customer Relationship Management Systems

A customer relationship management (CRM) system helps you manage and organize your interactions with clients and leads. It enables you to track your communications, keep detailed client profiles, and streamline your sales and marketing efforts. Consider the following benefits of utilizing a CRM system:

1. Efficient Data Management: A CRM system allows you to store and access client information in one centralized location. It makes it easier to track client interactions, access pertinent details, and maintain accurate records.

2. Streamlined Communication: With a CRM, you can schedule follow-up reminders, automate tasks, and even segment your contacts based on specific criteria. It helps ensure that you stay in regular communication with your clients and leads, increasing your efficiency and productivity.

3. Personalized Marketing: A CRM system can assist in creating targeted marketing campaigns. By segmenting contacts based on criteria such as location, interests, or buying behavior, you can send personalized messages that resonate with each group.

Automation Tools for Generating and Nurturing Leads

Automation tools can greatly streamline your lead generation and nurturing efforts. By automating repetitive tasks, you can save time and focus on more value-added activities. Consider the following automation tools:

1. Email Marketing Automation: Email marketing automation tools allow you to create email campaigns and set up automated sequences. You can send personalized email drips to leads and clients, nurturing them through the sales funnel automatically.

2. Social Media Management Tools: Social media management tools help schedule and automate your social media posts, saving you time and ensuring a consistent presence across platforms. You can also monitor and engage with social media conversations relevant to your business.

3. Lead Capture and Management Tools: These tools assist in capturing leads from various sources, such as your website or landing pages. They can also integrate with your CRM system, enabling you to track and manage leads efficiently.

Real Estate Investment Software

For real estate professionals involved in investment properties, utilizing real estate investment software can be highly beneficial. Such software provides tools and analysis to help identify profitable investment opportunities and manage portfolios effectively. Consider the following advantages:

1. Property Analysis: Real estate investment software offers tools to analyze potential properties, including rental income projections, expense tracking, and return on investment calculations. It helps you make informed investment decisions.

2. Portfolio Management: These software solutions often include features to manage and track multiple properties, their cash flow, and property-specific metrics. It streamlines communication with investors and facilitates reporting.

3. Market Research: Real estate investment software can provide access to market research data such as historical sales, rental rates, and forecasts. It helps you identify trends and make data-driven investment decisions.

In conclusion, leveraging technology in the real estate

industry can greatly enhance your productivity, efficiency, and effectiveness. Customer relationship management systems, automation tools for lead generation and nurturing, and real estate investment software are just a few examples of how technology can streamline your processes and drive success.

In the next chapter, we will explore the power of leveraging online reviews and testimonials to strengthen your reputation and attract more clients.

Chapter 10 –

Closing the Deal

In this chapter, we will explore strategies for effectively closing real estate deals. We will discuss techniques for engaging leads, best practices in converting leads into clients, and the importance of follow-ups. Let's get started!

Engaging a Lead Effectively

Engaging leads effectively is crucial to building rapport, understanding their needs, and ultimately closing the deal. Consider the following strategies:

1. Active Listening: Take the time to actively listen to your leads and understand their unique needs and preferences. Ask probing questions and show genuine interest in their requirements, allowing you to tailor your approach accordingly.

2. Provide Solutions: Position yourself as a problem solver by presenting suitable properties or options that align with your lead's criteria. Demonstrate your expertise and industry knowledge to instill trust and confidence.

3. Effective Communication: Communicate clearly and professionally, maintaining timely and responsive interactions. Use various mediums, such as phone calls, texts, emails, or video chats, to adapt to your lead's preferred mode of communication.

Best Practices in Converting Leads into Clients

Converting leads into clients requires a strategic approach to building trust and confidence. Consider the following best practices:

1. Build Relationships: Foster strong relationships with leads by consistently following up, attending to their inquiries promptly, and providing valuable information. Going above and beyond to address their concerns will help establish trust and increase the likelihood of conversion.

2. Create Urgency: Instill a sense of urgency by showcasing the unique value proposition of the property or opportunity. Highlight any time-sensitive factors or market trends that may motivate leads to take action quickly.

3. Offer Competitive Advantages: Clearly communicate the advantages of working with you, such as your expertise, market knowledge, or unique services. Differentiate yourself from competitors and create a compelling reason for leads to choose your services.

The Importance of Follow-ups

Follow-ups play a vital role in the closing process by nurturing relationships and staying top-of-mind with leads. Consider the following strategies for effective follow-ups:

1. Timeliness: Follow up promptly after initial interactions or property showings to maintain momentum and show your dedication. Prompt communication reinforces your commitment and professionalism.

2. Personalization: Tailor your follow-ups to each lead's needs and preferences. Reference specific details from previous conversations or interactions to demonstrate your attentiveness and personalized approach.

3. Persistence: Be persistent, but not pushy, in your follow-ups. Some leads may require more time or additional information before committing. Regularly check in, offer assistance, and provide valuable insights to keep them engaged.

In conclusion, closing real estate deals involves effectively engaging leads, converting them into clients through strategic practices, and maintaining consistent follow-ups. By employing these strategies, you can increase your chances of successfully closing deals and growing your real estate business.

In the next chapter, we will explore strategies for maintaining long-term client relationships and generating repeat business through exceptional customer service.

Chapter 11 –
The Future of Lead Generation

In this chapter, we will explore the future of lead generation in the real estate industry. We will discuss the role of artificial intelligence (AI) in lead generation, technological trends in real estate, and the importance of adapting to changing lead generation trends. Let's dive in!

The Role of Artificial Intelligence in Lead Generation

Artificial intelligence (AI) is playing an increasingly important role in lead generation. AI-powered tools and systems can automate and streamline processes, enabling real estate professionals to generate and nurture leads more efficiently. Consider the following aspects of AI in lead generation:

1. Lead Scoring and Prediction: AI can analyze vast amounts of data to score and predict lead quality and conversion likelihood. By leveraging machine learning algorithms, AI can identify patterns and prioritize high-potential leads, helping streamline the lead generation process.

2. Personalized Communication: AI-powered chatbots and virtual assistants can provide instant responses to inquiries and engage leads in real-time conversations. These automated systems can simulate human-like interactions, gather information, and provide personalized recommendations based on lead preferences.

Technological Trends in Real Estate

The real estate industry continues to evolve with technological advancements. Staying up-to-date with these trends can give you a competitive edge in lead generation. Consider the following technological trends:

1. Virtual and Augmented Reality: VR and AR technologies allow potential buyers to tour properties from the comfort of their own homes virtually. This immersive experience enhances the engagement and decision-making process, attracting highly interested leads.

In today's current economy, you as a realtor or anyone in the real estate business, are dealing with an extremely volatile industry. We cannot see into the future to plan for more uncertainty. The real estate markets are and have always been cyclical. It will get better, sooner or later. Confidence does not grow on trees. To build your confidence, you need someone who can always have your back. Jesus is someone you can turn to in difficult and challenging times. You can find help in God's Word.

Psalm 118:8: "*It is* better to trust in the LORD than to put confidence in man."

Don't take my word for it. Check out my accuracy by studying the Bible for yourself.

Psalm 118:9: "*It is* better to trust in the LORD than to put confidence in princes."

When you need help, do you trust the government to give you assistance? God says don't do that!

Proverbs 3:26: "For the LORD shall be thy confidence, and shall keep thy foot from being taken."

Proverbs 14:26: "In the fear of the LORD *is* strong confidence: and his children shall have a place of refuge."

Ephesians 3:11-12 "According to the eternal purpose which he purposed in Christ Jesus our Lord:

In whom we have boldness and access with confidence by the faith of him."

Technically, and in my opinion, the guidance you may desire from God is only available to those who trust in Him. Please take an honest look at your position in the realm of spirituality. Are you one of His children? Have you been "born again"? These are serious questions we all need to consider as we work towards a joyful ending in this life.

The End (or is this just the beginning?)

www.ingramcontent.com/pod-product-compliance
Lightning Source LLC
Chambersburg PA
CBHW060259030426
42335CB00014B/1773